Deirdre the Iris

MW01672875

Deirdre's costumes are on Plates 7 to 14.

Deirdre

Diana

Diana the Classical Ballerina

Diana's costumes are on Plates 15 to 22.

Kati the Nutcracker Ballerina

Kati's costumes are on Plates 23 to 30.

Kati

Kimberly

Kimberly the Little Ballerina

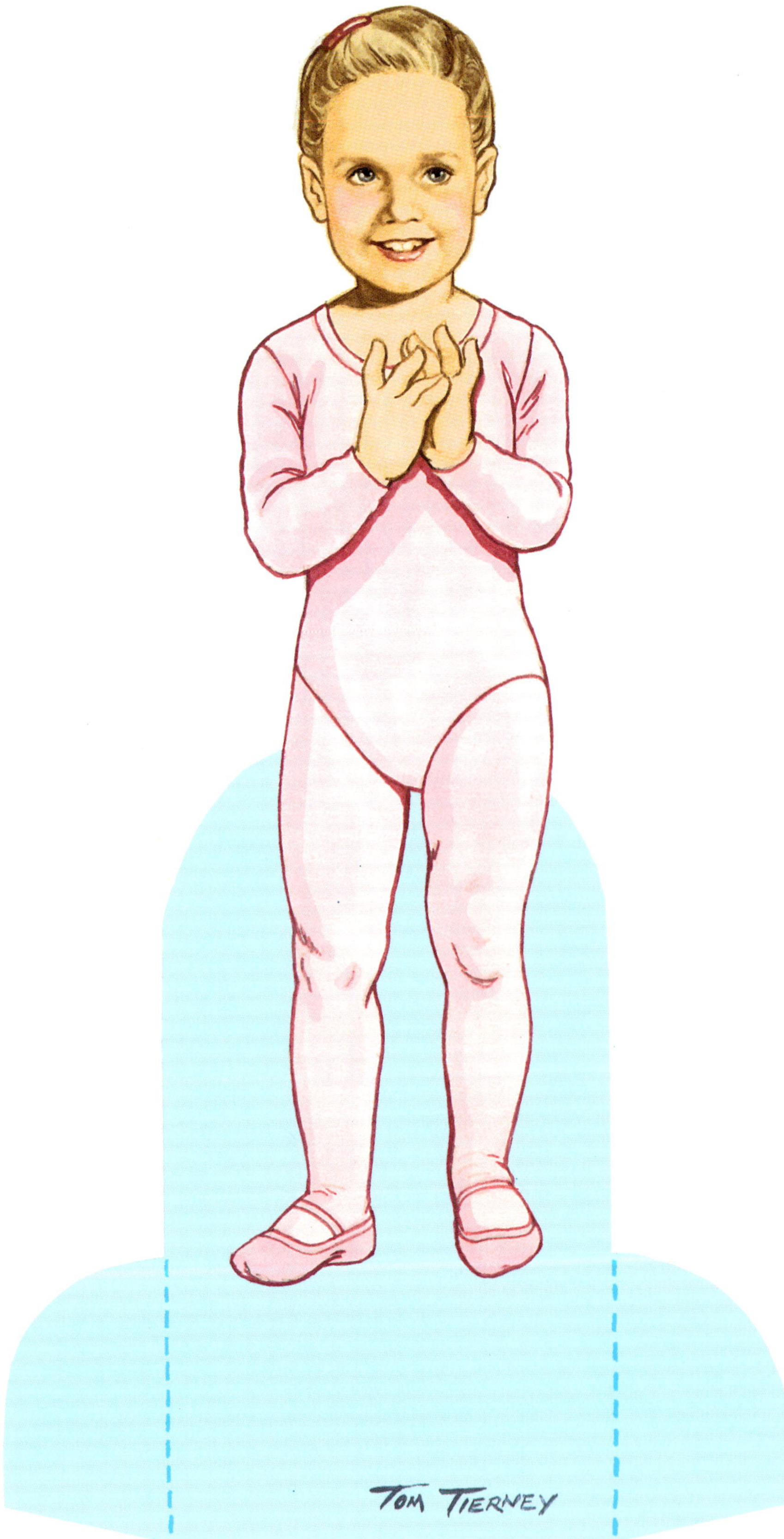

Kimberly's costumes are on Plates 31 to 38.

Megan the Prima Ballerina

Megan's costumes are on Plates 39 to 46.

Megan

Melissa

Melissa the Fairy Ballerina

Melissa's costumes are on Plates 47 to 54.

Deirdre the Irish Dancer

Deirdre

Irish Dancer

Deirdre

Irish Dancer

Deirdre the Irish Dancer

cut on dashed line

Deirdre the Irish Dancer

Deirdre

Irish Dancer

Deirdre

Irish Dancer

Deirdre the Irish Dancer

Deirdre the Irish Dancer

Deirdre

Irish Dancer

Deirdre

Irish Dancer

Deirdre the Irish Dancer

Deirdre the Irish Dancer

Deirdre

Irish Dancer

Deirdre

Irish Dancer

Deirdre the Irish Dancer

Diana the Classical Ballerina

cut on dashed line

Diana

Le Pas de Quatre

Diana

Petrouchka

Diana the Classical Ballerina

Petrouchka

Diana the Classical Ballerina

cut on dashed line

Blue Bird from *Sleeping Beauty*

Diana

Blue Bird
from
Sleeping Beauty

Diana

Don Quixote

Diana the Classical Ballerina

Don Quixote

Diana the Classical Ballerina

Snowflake from *The Nutcracker*

Diana

Snowflake
from
The Nutcracker

Diana

Clara
from
The Nutcracker

Diana the Classical Ballerina

Clara from *The Nutcracker*

Diana the Classical Ballerina

Waltz of the Flowers from *The Nutcracker*

Diana

Waltz of the Flowers
from
The Nutcracker

Diana

Firebird

Diana the Classical Ballerina

Firebird

Kati the Nutcracker Ballerina

cut on dashed line

Clara's party dress
(holding Nutcracker doll)

Kati

Clara's party dress
(holding Nutcracker doll)
from *The Nutcracker*

Kati

Mechanical Doll
from *The Nutcracker*

Kati the Nutcracker Ballerina

Mechanical Doll

Kati the Nutcracker Ballerina

Columbine

Kati

Columbine from
The Nutcracker

Kat

Kati

A Warrior Mouse from
The Nutcracker

Kati the Nutcracker Ballerina

A Warrior Mouse

Kati the Nutcracker Ballerina

Clara in the Forest

Kati

Clara in the Forest from
The Nutcracker

Kati

The Sugar Plum Fairy
from *The Nutcracker*

Kati the Nutcracker Ballerina

The Sugar Plum Fairy

Kati the Nutcracker Ballerina

Spanish Chocolate

Kati

Spanish Chocolate
from *The Nutcracker*

Kati

Mother Ginger
(with peppermint children)
from *The Nutcracker*

Kati the Nutcracker Ballerina

Mother Ginger
(with peppermint children)

Kimberly the Little Ballerina

Do not cut out white areas between arms and body.

Rehearsal Clothes

Kimberly

Rehearsal Clothes

Kimberly

"Dance of the Clowns"

Kimberly the Little Ballerina

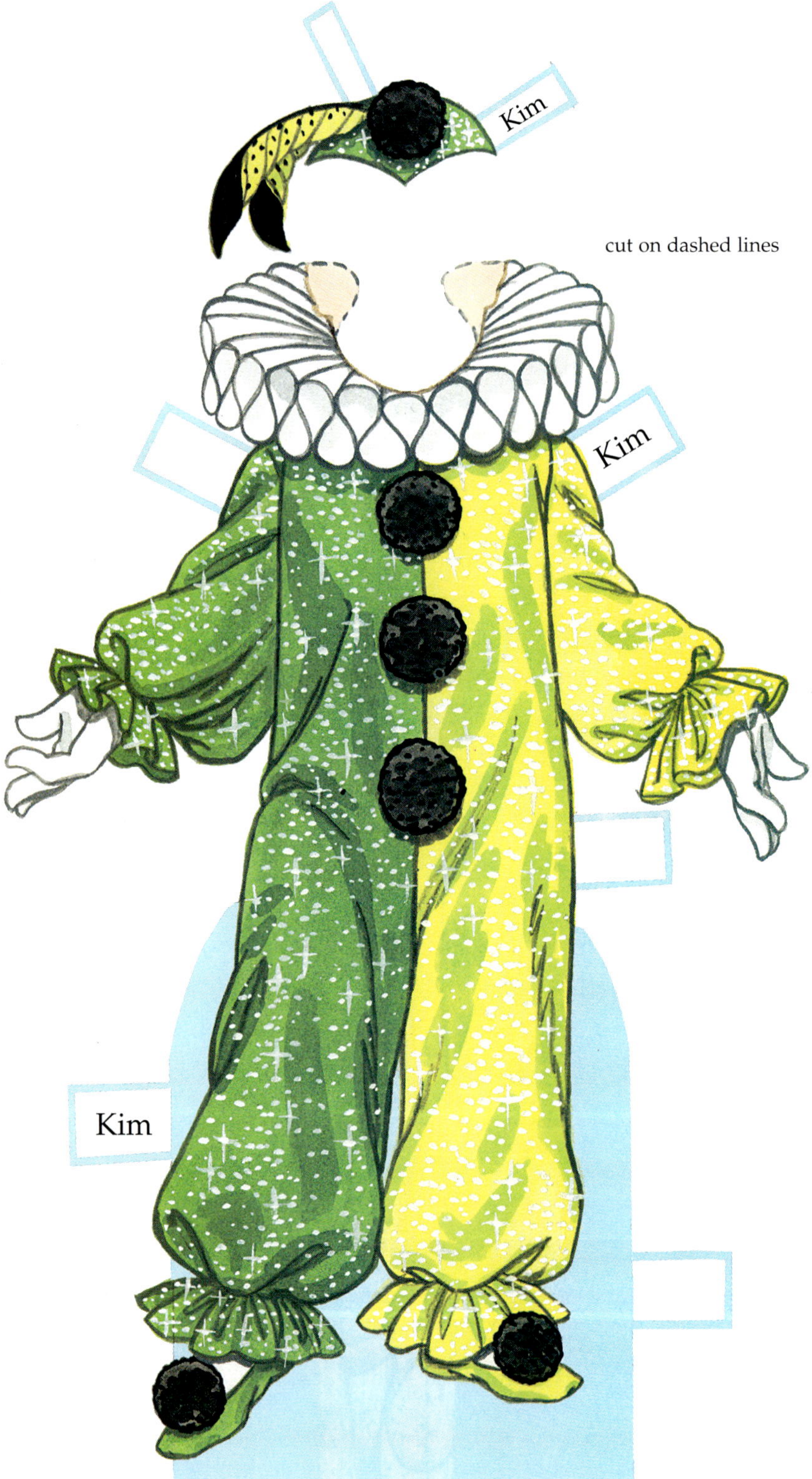

"Dance of the Clowns"

"Ballet Folkloric"

Kim

Kimberly

"Ballet Folkloric"

Kimberly

"Little Princess"

Kimberly the Little Ballerina

"Little Princess"

Kimberly the Little Ballerina

"Kitty Capers"

Kim

Kimberly

"Kitty Capers"

Kimberly

"Toy Shop Jamboree"

Kimberly the Little Ballerina

"Toy Shop Jamboree"

Kimberly the Little Ballerina

Do not cut out white area between arm and body.

"Little Starlight Fairy"

Kim

Kimberly

"Little Starlight Fairy"

Kim

Kimberly

"Yankee Doodle Dandy"

Kimberly the Little Ballerina

cut on dashed line

Do not cut out white areas between arms and body.

"Yankee Doodle Dandy"

Megan the Prima Ballerina

cut on dashed lines

Giselle

Megan

Giselle

Meg

Megan

Odette from *Swan Lake*

Megan the Prima Ballerina

Odette from *Swan Lake*

Megan the Prima Ballerina

Odile from *Swan Lake*

Megan

Odile from *Swan Lake*

Meg

Megan

Swanilda from *Coppelia*

Megan the Prima Ballerina

Swanilda from *Coppelia*

Megan the Prima Ballerina

Cinderella (in rags)

Megan

Cinderella (in rags)

Megan

Cinderella (in riches)

Megan the Prima Ballerina

cut on dashed lines

Cinderella (in riches)

Megan the Prima Ballerina

Princess Aurora from *Sleeping Beauty*

Meg

Megan

Princess Aurora from
Sleeping Beauty

Megan

Clara from
The Nutcracker

Megan the Prima Ballerina

cut on dashed lines

Clara from *The Nutcracker*

Melissa the Fairy Ballerina

The Sugar Plum Fairy from
The Nutcracker

Mel

Melissa

The Sugar Plum Fairy
from *The Nutcracker*

Mel

Melissa

Fairy of the Crystal
Fountain from
Sleeping Beauty

Melissa the Fairy Ballerina

Fairy of the Crystal Fountain
from *Sleeping Beauty*

Melissa the Fairy Ballerina

The Lilac Fairy from
Sleeping Beauty

Mel

Melissa

The Lilac Fairy from *Sleeping Beauty*

Melissa

La Péri

Melissa the Fairy Ballerina

La Péri

Melissa the Fairy Ballerina

Queen of the Wilis from *Giselle*

Melissa

Queen of the Wilis from *Giselle*

Melissa

The Fairy Godmother
from *Cinderella*

Melissa the Fairy Ballerina

The Fairy Godmother
from *Cinderella*

Melissa the Fairy Ballerina

Titania from *A Midsummer Night's Dream*

Melissa

Titania from
A Midsummer
Night's Dream

Mel

Melissa

La Sylphide

Melissa the Fairy Ballerina

La Sylphide